# WASHINGTON II

# WASHINGTON II

PHOTOGRAPHY BY RAY ATKESON

TEXT BY ARCHIE SATTERFIELD

GRAPHIC ARTS CENTER PUBLISHING COMPANY

PORTLAND, OREGON

# CONTENTS

International Standard Book Number 0-912856-12-2
Library of Congress Catalog Number 70-81401
Copyright© 1973 by Graphic Arts Center Publishing Co.
P.O. Box 10306 • Portland, Oregon 97210 • 503/226-2402
Designer • Robert Reynolds
Typography • Paul O. Giesey/Adcrafters
Printer • Graphic Arts Center
Binding • Lincoln & Allen
Printed in the United States of America
Ninth Printing

Page ii: Wild rhododendron, state flower of Washington.

Right: Low-hanging clouds drift across the slopes of Wilmon Peaks above glacier-fed stream in Monte Cristo region of North Cascades.

A Columbian blacktail deer strolls leisurely along the
crest of Hurricane Ridge in Olympic National Park.

Aerial view of Deep Lake in Sun Lakes State Park.
On pages 4 and 5 following: View from Steptoe Butte,
a springtime panorama of grain fields in the
Palouse Country.

Left: Colorful lava flows tiered in layers tower above
Lenore Lake in Grand Coulee area.

Morning sun illuminates the upper reaches of Mt. Baker
in the Cascade Range. View from Kulshan Ridge.

The Washougal River, popular recreational
tributary of the Columbia River.

Yale Lake and Mount St. Helens with steam rising
from crater.

Right: Thunder Creek Arm on Diablo Lake in Ross Lake National Recreation Area. In background, Colonial Peak.

Delicate fall colors reflected on the mirror-like surface of Sullivan Lake.

Left: Reflection Lake mirrors the glacier-clad dome of
Mt. Rainier in Mt. Rainier National Park.

Aerial view of Roche Harbor on San Juan Island.

Asparagus field reared in the fertile soil
of the Touchet River Valley.

Stately Douglas Fir reflects the environment surrounding Lake Crescent in Olympic National Park.

Left: Liberty Bell soars high above the new North
Cascades Highway as it climbs up to Washington Pass.

Wild flowers carpet the slopes of Hurricane Ridge at
the base of the snow-crested Olympic Mountains.

Left: Midday sun creates spectacular burst atop snow-covered conifer in the White Pass ski area.

Sunset gives brilliant color to a cloud-filled sky over the southern coast. On pages 20 and 21 following: Offshore winds spin off crest of wave as it rolls toward southern coast.

Autumn-colored aspen near Tonasket.

## THE WASHINGTON EXPERIENCE

Great things have been expected of Washington in the 150-odd years since the settlers arrived and shunted aside the Indians and their society based on environmental pragmatism. Many of the newcomers believed this far corner of the land with its rivers and trees and mountains and plains and saltwater beaches could produce a more superior form of American society. It was the last part of the nation to be settled and the 19th Century dreamers thought it was the nation's last chance. Perhaps more important, they tended to believe man and nature were the sole components of the whole universe. They saw this area in its totally natural condition, the forests intact, the streams clean and free-flowing, the lakes pristine and, to complete the natural setting, one of the four volcanoes, Mount St. Helens, was still smoking.

They prophesied the West would be the cradle of a new, more flexible democracy. Early poets believed an age was at hand when men of the West, and particularly the "Oregon Country," would yield to their natural environment and learn to live at peace with their surroundings and each other. By contrast, present poets of the old Oregon Country know better, and their work is almost uniformly somber.

But the newcomers had their hopes, just as today's migrants to Washington initially assume the natural setting will make Washington a better place to live than their previous address. Some are disappointed; most are not.

Today we can only imagine what a beautiful land it must have been when the first paradise seekers arrived. It is not in the American tradition to leave things as they are, and the results of our manipulation of Washington's original appearance has turned the state into something of a grab bag. While industrialists and naturalists have not learned peaceful coexistence, they have frequently stalemated each other on unreasonable demands. There are jobs for people and scenery to enjoy in their leisure time.

It is indicative of the quality of Washington's residents that nearly every county has a historical society, and that many small towns have begun retaining their individuality and are attempting to re-establish themselves as separate entities. Several have declared their independence from the down-at-heels appearance that plagues so many towns and have started restoring businesses to their appearance when the town was founded. Leavenworth was a forerunner in this emphasis on small-town integrity when it redesigned the entire business district into a Bavarian theme, began a series of seasonal festivals and became known throughout the nation as a small town with style.

During the past decade several bitter environmental battles have been fought in Western Washington. Despite claims to the contrary at the time of the battles, few today will deny the state is a better, a healthier and more beautiful place to live with cleaner streams, purer air and natural scenery rather than an industrial wasteland. The quality of life, a nebulous concept with a definition varying from man to man, remains high in Washington.

Most attention on the quality of life has been focused on the western part of the state because the majority of its residents live there, and its industrial development has been heaviest.

While farmers have often been the butt of city jokes, there aren't many jokes told about Eastern Washington farmers, unless it is their generally conservative approach to life which to metropolitan liberals appears regressive. But while environmental battles were big news in the Puget Sound Basin, the farmers continued going their usual way—planting crops in fall or the spring, cultivating and harvesting them in the summer and fall. Environmentally, farmers must be pragmatic or perish. They must take excellent care of the land or it will not function for them. For years the farmers burned wheat stubble after harvest, until they discovered it should be plowed back into the soil to help hold moisture in the ground, and to keep the topsoil from blowing away during windstorms. They also shot every coyote and hawk they could. But when they found those so-called enemies killed their actual enemies—field mice and other rodents—the killing stopped. Still unresolved is the matter of chemical weed killers. Agricultural scientists such as Nobel prize winner Norman Bourlag have been conducting research on the chemicals to determine how much, if any, of the poisons actually appear in the finished food product.

Another barometer of Washingtonians' love for the land is their efforts to discourage immigration. Unlike the national immigration policies based on racial prejudice, political expediency or bureaucratic quirks, the majority of people in Washington know that the quality of life diminishes as the ratio of persons per square mile increases. They freely admit to selfishness when their favorite steelhead bar becomes crowded or when their backpacking trails become a maze of bootprints. They tend to resist tourist-promotion schemes (except those communities whose livelihood depends directly on tourism) and they fight real estate developments in prime recreational or scenic areas.

Those opposed to further immigration into the state have not yet followed the example of Oregon, which has a hardy band of tourist and immigrant opponents.

In 1874 there appeared in *Harper's New Monthly Magazine* a delightful report by Charles Nordhoff on a trip through the Washington Territory. It must have stung readers here when it appeared, and even today would not be accepted locally by anti-growth proponents because it pokes fun at the state's penchant for names difficult to pronounce. Also, it was written by one of those "superior" Easterners who have seldom been well accepted in the Northwest.

"When, at Kalama," Nordhoff wrote, "you enter Washington Territory, your ears begin to be assailed by the most barbarous names imaginable. On your way to Olympia by rail you cross a river called the Skookum-Chuck; your train stops at places named Newaukum, Tumwater, and Toutle; and if you seek further, you will hear of whole counties labeled Wahkiakum, or Snohomish, or Kitsar (Kitsap), or Klikatat (sic) and Cowlitz, Hookium, and Nenolelops greet and offend you. They complain in Olympia that Washington Territory gets but little immigration; but what wonder? What man, having the whole American continent to choose from, would willingly date his letters from the county of Snohomish, or bring up his children in the city of Nenolelops? The village of Tumwater is, as I am ready to bear witness, very pretty indeed; but surely an emigrant would think twice before he established himself either there or at Toutle. Seattle is sufficiently barbarous; Steilacoom is no better; and I suspect that the Northern Pacific Railroad terminus has been fixed at Tacoma because it is one of the few places on Puget

Sound whose name does not inspire horror and disgust." Nordhoff surely knew better than to make another visit to Washington Territory. There is no record of his being lynched, so he apparently let one visit suffice. He did comment on the beauty here, but he failed to see any further into the future than the next stop on his tour.

The concern for the quality of life in Washington maintained its momentum even when the unemployment rate was the highest in the nation. The core of preservationists continued the battle for protection of nature, and many families with no job prospects preferred remaining in Washington with lower-paying jobs than moving to another part of the country for an income comparable to what they once had here.

Living in Washington, then, is a way of life that may not be wholly unique, but it is quite special. It is not a hard land, and it has not developed a hard people. It has produced more national figures in the conservation movement than any other state, and some of the most important battles over environmental protection and aesthetic preservation have been waged here. The conservation movement dates back to before the turn of the century with the establishment of Mount Rainier National Park and proposals of a series of parks in the Cascade Range. The conservation cause was a way of life, a calling if you prefer, long before the sophisticated terms of environmentalist or ecologist came into common usage. Those living up to the definition of those words have learned to live with the double standard of their enemies—those who wouldn't consider living in any other part of the land, but also have a compulsion to change the face of that land they love so dearly.

This concern for nature, which may appear somewhat extreme to outsiders unfamiliar with the state's diversity and the infinite variety of personal experiences it offers, actually makes more sense than might be visible on the surface. The forces of nature have been remarkably kind to the state, in spite of violent geologic history of volcanoes, jutting mountains and the scrape and grind of the Ice Age.

Here it is the wind, the rain and the mountains—three natural forces that form a relationship not unlike 18th Century music and poetry, a rigid structure with infinite variations. In the west it is the Olympics, then the Cascades that transform the moist winds off the Pacific into rain and snow. There are places beneath the Olympic Mountains that receive more than 200 inches of rainfall a year, just as there are places 200 miles away that receive fewer than 10 inches a year. As one crosses the state east to west, the change in plant life is obvious as one nears the Cascades. Mile by mile the trees become larger and closer together, the underbrush thicker and more luxuriant. Rainfall charts show a stairstep increase in inches a year as the graph lines approach the summit of the range.

The state is also a result of the prevailing winds out of the southwest, steady in their course and almost as predictable as the tides. For eons those winds have brought the soil, or loess, to Eastern Washington. Like the rain from the Pacific, over the centuries it has fallen steadily across the scabland, down into the coulees, on the high plains and the steep, rolling hills of the Palouse. Like driven snow, it has accumulated deeper on the southwest edges of buttes and hills, leaving some north slopes barren of productive soil. Its annual accumulation is measured in tons an acre,

and in some places it is more than 200 feet deep. With the limited but dependable rainfall, the soil has made the Palouse Country along the Idaho border the richest wheat-growing land on the face of the earth.

The Cascades also divide the state so completely that it often has been suggested the crest of the range would have made a more sensible boundary for the state. The division goes much deeper than geography. It is an industrial, political, cultural and emotional line between the halves. The state's cultural and geographic diversity is at once its political weakness and its scenic and recreational strength. The one-man, one-vote concept of political science was expensive for the rural eastern half of the state, but with the growth of agriculture in the Columbia Basin and the supporting industries, the population appears to be slowly shifting, attempting to balance itself.

Although the state is neatly divided by the crest of the Cascade Range, there are some rather obvious subdivisions within those halves. They offer a diversity of scenery and culture that is the envy of other states. It is a major reason many people do not feel compelled to spend their vacation budgets in other states and countries: It is surprising how many Washingtonians do not cross the state lines for vacations. They have the desert, the saltwater beaches, the mountains, the cities, the trails, the fishing streams and lakes—virtually anything offered by other Western states.

They can spend a weekend or a vacation on the Long Beach Peninsula and find reasonable motel and restaurant rates even at the height of the tourist season. On one side of the long, sandy peninsula are the sand dunes, the saltwater and headlands with small coves for beachcombing and picnicking. On the opposite side is Willapa Bay, the last undeveloped major estuary on the West Coast and one of the most beautiful. In the middle of Willapa Bay is the Long Island Wildlife Refuge for the endangered black brant, other migratory waterfowl, deer, raccoon and other wildlife.

History is as much a part of the Long Beach Peninsula as its usually wet weather. Lewis and Clark camped there before giving up and crossing the Columbia River to a site near Astoria. The town of Chinook, obviously named for the species of salmon, at one time was the major salmon-seining grounds on the West Coast. Horses were trained to wade in the mixture of river and saltwater, pulling long seines and hauling in salmon by the ton. The town is small, modest and unobtrusive today, but only five or six decades ago it boasted the highest per capita income of any city in the nation.

Today the Chinook-Ilwaco area is better known as a charter-boat fishing resort than a commercial fishing port, and motel managers spend much of their lives rising in the small hours of the morning to wake their guests in time to catch the boats headed for the fishing grounds.

History also is evident in less pleasant reminders, such as the wrecks of ships dating from last winter to last century that line the coastline on either side of the Columbia's estuary. With good reason that area has been named the "Graveyard of the Pacific" with maps showing the location of more than 100 shipwrecks.

The Columbia from the sea upstream to Bonneville Dam near Vancouver is called the Lower Columbia, a broad stretch of water that fluctuates with the tides. The air along the wide river has a tangy smell and taste, and oceangoing ships ply the river as matter-of-factly as they do Puget Sound. The lives of fishermen along this portion of the river are governed by the tides which halt, then reverse the flow of the mighty river. Towboats and tugs cannot work upstream during an outgoing tide because the normal speed of the river and the dropping tide creates a current too swift for headway with a load.

The people living along the river's edge are for the most part first and second generation immigrants. Most came from the Scandinavian countries, with a few Swiss and Germans scattered through the area. Some have never bothered to learn fluent English because it was not required where neighbors speak the same European language. They were fishermen, loggers, farmers or cannery workers. The area was not served by adequate roads until after World War II, and many alive remember catching the steamboats that had scheduled runs from Astoria to Portland. The gillnet boats then were equipped with sails, and people still tell of the pretty sight sailboats made when they came into Gray's Bay after a day on the river.

Further east, behind the dams which turned the Columbia into a series of lakes, the Columbia loses its character as a river. Boaters and swimmers enjoy the change; environmental purists do not and they are fighting a plan to dam the last stretch of free-flowing river in Central Washington. The slackwater has almost entirely changed the character of the Columbia Gorge so that one must look to the cliffs lining the river now for exciting scenery—waterfalls, wind-sculpted cliffs and so forth. Gone perhaps forever are The Cascades, The Dalles, Celilo Falls. Mourners of their passing decrease as the decades pass.

North of the river are several sections of extreme beauty, such as the Camas Valley and the Klickitat Valley. Picturesque farms, often with Mount Adams, Mount St. Helens and Mount Rainier on view, make these among the most beautiful farming areas in the state. A little further north is the Yakima River Valley, at one time a rushing river bordered by barren hills. But the introduction of irrigation has changed the valley into one of the prime agricultural areas of the state with orchards, hop farms, vineyards, row-crop farms and some grain farms.

In order to fully appreciate the Columbia Basin, the vast irrigated midsection of the state, one should see photographs of the area before Grand Coulee Dam was completed, and talk to the people who lived there before the dam was completed. The most widely quoted description is "wind, sagebrush and rattlesnakes." Before irrigation, the area teetered on the edge of being a true desert. Rainfall was negligible, and any farming attempted was a high-risk proposition. Many tried it but few succeeded. About the only thing the land would support was cattle, but then only in terms of several acres per cow.

The Grand Coulee Dam changed all that, and in the process almost completely altered the face of the land. Canyons which once were filled with water behind the receding Ice Age glaciers were again filled with Columbia River water pumped from the dam. It was sent by ditches and tunnels, or siphons, across the land, turning half a million acres into one of the greatest agricultural areas in North America. It appears anything that will grow in a moderate climate grows profusely in the Columbia Basin. One has only to drive along the border of the irrigation project to see the

change it has made. On one side of the road will be green vegetables, on the other side will be barren ground with an occasional sprig of sagebrush or Canadian thistle.

East of the Columbia Basin farms lie what is generally referred to as the Wheat Country. Some deep-well irrigation has been established there, but for the most part it still is semiarid farming. Directly east of the Columbia Basin the rainfall is in the range of 8 to 12 inches annually. Not much, but enough to grow good stands of wheat. With the predictable rainfall, the absence of excessive hailstorms, seldom any rain during the crucial harvest time and other blights to wheat farmers on the Great Plains, the yield is steady if not spectacular.

Somewhere less than 100 miles from the Idaho border the Palouse Country begins. No one can draw an accurate map of the Palouse Country's eastern boundary, but to a wheat farmer it means both more rainfall a year and the steep, low hills for which the region was named. The land has a slight upward tilt to it as one moves east, and at the state-line city of Pullman, the elevation is more than 2,000 feet. This accounts for the increase in rainfall which in turn yields up to 100 bushels of wheat an acre with 60 bushels considered only an adequate year. Back over in the semiarid wheat land, the average is closer to 25-30 bushels an acre.

The general north-south boundaries of the Palouse are from the Snake River north to the Spokane Valley. North of the Spokane Valley the hills become steeper, rock outcrops more frequent and the hills timbered with pine. Farther north of Spokane toward the Canadian border logging and mining are more dominant than other areas of Eastern Washington, and near the town of Republic is the state's only operating gold mine. The gold-mining heritage of the town and surrounding area is reflected in its choice of names for streets and business that represent great gold rushes, such as Klondike.

West of Spokane is one of the state's most popular playgrounds, also a result of Grand Coulee Dam. Its backwaters, Roosevelt Lake, are one of the West's prime boating areas and the lake is so vast that one can always find secluded coves for camping from boats.

The Okanogan Country in North-Central Washington is another broad expanse of rolling, open country in some ways more Western than the more familiar western states. Cattle ranches, cattle drives in the spring and fall, and the Omak Stampede, one of the wildest of the rodeos, give the area an atmosphere of bow legs and creaking saddles. The small town of Winthrop is one of the later additions to the growing list of towns with ambitious restoration and theme projects. Methow is a town of false-front buildings, hitching posts, horse troughs and swinging-door saloons. The town's isolation was ended when the North Cascades Highway was completed in 1972, giving the state five cross-state highways. The tourist business will undoubtedly grow in the Okanogan Country, to the pleasure of some businessmen and to the despair of the status-quo set.

Probably no part of the state has caused more words to be set in type than the Cascade Range. It long has been a battleground over preservation versus logging and mining. It is the summer playground for hikers and boaters, and the winter-sports capital of the Pacific Northwest. Ski resorts, housing developments and snowshoe trails compete with logging roads and the tree cutters for the beautiful mountain range. With the North Cascades National Park, covering more than 500,000 acres is the Passayten Wilderness Area, Mount Rainier National Park, Goat Rocks Wilderness Area, Mount Adams Wilderness Area, the Cougar Lakes Wilderness Area and other smaller wilderness enclaves. A proposal under study at this writing would, if successful, create a new wilderness area, the Alpine Lakes, surrounded by a buffer zone of a national recreational area. The two areas would total some 900,000 acres dedicated to recreational uses.

Western Washington above the Long Beach Peninsula can be divided into two general geographic and cultural areas: the Washington coast and the Puget Sound Basin. One, the coast, is still wild and intentionally untamed, and the other is largely urbanized.

The Washington coast above the resort areas of Grays Harbor and Ocean Shores has remained relatively untouched due to the ocean corridor added to the Olympic National Park and the Quinault Indian Reservation. Storms are more common there than sunny, still days and the shoreline is marked by jutting headlands, offshore rocks, occasional flat beaches and dense forests behind the beach sand. No highway traverses the coast, and it is unlikely one ever will. It has been left to the lovers of nature in the raw, sea gulls, sea lions, clams, starfish and an occasional shipwreck. There are many who believe the Washington coast, because it is so wild and so stormy much of the time, is the most beautiful coastline in America. But those accustomed to scenery with a maximum of comfort are not that impressed.

Directly behind the coast is the magnificent Olympic National Park with its moss-laden rain forests, glacier-scarred peaks, sudden open valleys and incredibly blue lakes. The park is something of an everyman's recreation area with trails ranging from five-minute strolls to tough ascents for the experienced rock climber only. It is one place in the West where one can see stunning scenery without leaving the car, which makes it particularly appealing for the elderly or the handicapped.

For years there have been frequent and dire predictions about the coming of a Pugetopolis, an arrow-shaped city running from Vancouver, Washington, to the Canadian border along the route of Interstate 5. There is some justification, obviously, for this prediction. Western Washington, and particularly the Puget Sound basin from Olympia to Blaine, has been addicted to industrial growth and the accompanying population expansion. The Chambers of Commerce are committed to the growth concept ("grow or perish") while others, the environmentalists and intellectuals, have fought the program.

Puget Sound shows signs of wear and tear from overuse by people and misuse by industrial interests. Most of its shoreline is in private ownership and its beaches closed to the general public. Only at a selected few spots can one park the car and walk on the beach without fear of being told to leave ("This is private property, mister!"). In spite of this, it still is a lovely body of water, one of the most beautiful sounds in the world. It is a combination playground for the boating fraternity and workshop for the shipping interests. Small sailboats and gigantic freighters passing within a few feet of each other are common sights to Puget Sound watchers.

At its upper boundary lie the gems of the Pacific Northwest, the San Juan Islands. Relatively isolated from the rest of the state—the rest of the world, some say—the islands have for years represented the ultimate in escape without going to Tahiti. They have farms on them, an occasional cattle ranch, and some of the smaller islands are owned by state or federal agencies and managed as parks and wilderness preserves. Difficult and expensive to get to, the islands have been able to maintain most of their remoteness without succumbing to vast population gains, the instant slums of shoddy real estate promotions and bridges from the mainland.

This, then, is an overview of Washington. Some say it is so divided by the mountain range that it is schizophrenic. Others say that is its strength. But the undeniable fact about its scenery and the constituency is that it will fight, at the drop of a call for construction bids, to keep that scenery intact.

The citizens who chose Washington as a place to live may be a disappointment to those 19th Century poets and prophets because its people aren't that much different and the state laws are no more enlightened than a dozen other states. Perhaps man is

*European artisans used their skills to create a bit of Bavaria at Leavenworth in the foothills of the Cascade Range.*

immune to the inarticulate urges brought on by natural beauty; scenery alone cannot influence genes. But it has had its effect in more subtle ways, among them that refusal of many to leave here only for the sake of more money and that selfishness residents feel about sharing the beauty with more newcomers.

In an era of deep concern for nonrenewable resources, there are many in Washington who believe personal experience also is a renewable resource, that some of those experiences are worthy of being handed down from generation to generation as an item of cultural value. They want their children to know the thrill of a cross-country ski trip in the Cascades, a steelheading trip down the Skagit River, the terror of being caught on a high, bare ridge when the electrically charged air stands the hair on end and the smell of ozone is heavy in the air, the quietness of a summer dawn on Roosevelt Lake, the solitude of trolling for salmon in Puget Sound, the claustrophobia of a coastal rain forest, the sound of silence after shutting down a tractor and the southwest wind dies for the day.

These things matter in Washington. They are part of our culture.

On page 27 preceding: Autumn-tinted huckleberry
and mountain ash border tiny Sunrise Lake in Mt. Baker
National Forest. Grain elevators dominate
the skyline in Pomeroy.

Stately old trees drop their autumn foliage in a
Walla Walla residential area.

Autumn sunset illuminates the barren hills along
the Snake River near Clarkston.

Brilliant sunset reflected on the tranquil surface of
Pend Oreille Lake, Idaho. Lakes of Northern
Idaho and Northeastern Washington are favorite
playgrounds of Inland Empire.

Right: Sunlight reflections pierce the forested slopes
of Swift Reservoir on the Lewis River.

The road to the crest of Slate Mountain (elevation
7,488 feet) in the Okanagon National Forest.

Sunset reflection on the Columbia River
between Pasco and Kennewick.

Elk herd on snow-covered eastern slopes of the
Cascade Range near Yakima. On pages 36 and 37
following: Late afternoon view from crest of Steptoe
Butte captures the beautiful undulations
of the Palouse grain fields.

An Indian Summer morning at Liberty Lake
near Spokane.

The town of Colville nestled in a delightful valley.

Interstate Highway 82 climbs over rolling hills
overlooking the fertile Kittitas Valley.

Combine harvests a field of wheat on the rolling
terrain of Skyrocket Hills near Waitsburg.

Right: View from Kamiak Butte State Park across the golden grain fields of the Palouse region. On the horizon, historic Steptoe Butte.

Snow-capped Mt. Spokane above the autumn-fringed waters of Spirit Lake in Idaho.

Flowering plants herald the coming of spring
on the rugged hills overlooking the
Columbia River at Wallula Gap.

Evergreen forests surround the numerous
farms in the Colville Valley.

Summer Falls thunders over lava wall into
Long Lake in the Columbia Basin.

Mill Creek from its source in the Blue Mountains
flows through grove of cottonwood near Walla Walla.

Right: Wild flowers in foothills of the Cascade Range;
Avalanche Lily, Grass Widow, Yellow Bells.
Porcupine Creek in the North Cascade Range.

Golden-tinted larch trees (commonly called tamaracks)
weave a mosaic pattern through a dense pine forest
above Heritage Lake.

Mt. Shuksan (elevation 9,127 feet) in North Cascades National Park. View from Table Mountain in Mt. Baker National Forest.

## THE MIGRATION

The old houses lie scattered across Central and Eastern Washington, empty, wallpaper peeling and crumbling to the warped floor, the fine woodwork stripped and the linoleum rotted by rain and snow. Birds nest in the eaves and corners of the rooms. Field mice scurry through them and an occasional snake slithers across the floor in search of living food. Urban photographers and painters love them and architects buy their cured boards that look so rustic in dens and family rooms.

Outside will be a snag of a windmill, sometimes a few blades still intact and the vane creaking uselessly in the wind. Depending on the year of its desertion, or the whims of the last occupant, an outhouse may still stand. A few hardy flowers will return each spring, usually irises or lilies. But most of the yard will be plowed and crops planted, all roads and paths obliterated, the house now an island surrounded by a rolling sea of soil.

A barn or machine shed may still stand and inside will be a scattering of useless pieces of harness, some stripped bolts and odd-sized nuts, holes in the greasy work bench where the vise and the anvil were anchored. There may be names or dates burned into the beams with a white-hot steel rod cooked in the small portable forge. You can tell where the forge stood; it was surrounded by the black clinkers still scattered in one corner. The windows will be broken, some neatly drilled and spider-webbed by rifle slugs.

But it is the house that attracts us, and each is the biography of a family. No farm home is built with temporary occupancy in mind. The beams and rafters will be sturdy, the studs close together, the floors sound and thick. The outward appearance might not please modern architects and it may at best be called Pioneer Eclectic, or more sarcastically, an architectural abortion. But the total effect to those not concerned with trends is one of stability. The house may be lacking in subtlety but it was built for the generations. Even with no upkeep, it will endure. It will endure for decades to come, untended and taken for granted by local people, admired by outsiders. It will endure only as long as the ground beneath it is not valuable enough to cultivate.

Each of these homes has a name, always from one of the owners and usually the original owner, and always a place—the Schmidt Place, the Bronson Place, the Culpepper Place. These names affix for all time a geographic location on the map of one's homeland and the roots of a family tree. It is a genetic history, the record of human endeavor and an integral part of the place one knows best.

They became "ghost houses" for various reasons, just as whole communities become ghost towns: The couple had no children and when they retired they sold the land to a neighbor. The farm changed ownership several times, beginning in the Great Depression, but always retained its original name. The owners' children became urbanites—engineers, teachers, attorneys and physicians. The farm is still owned by the family estate and worked on a share-cropper basis by another farmer, one-third of the gross to the estate, two-thirds to the share-cropper. The owners moved to town and commute to the farm to have the advantage of town life while remaining farmers.

Gradually the size of the farms has increased while the number of individually owned farms decreased.

It is called economics, or agri-business. Farms, like industries, have had to grow both in the number of acres and investment in equipment or they will die in the bankruptcy courts. The trend has been the same in the Columbia Basin irrigation project, originally designed to put a large number of farmers on smaller plots of new land. There, they have changed ownership, more successful farmers consolidating, expanding, experimenting with new crops. The vast grazing lands of the Basin, with an occasional ranch house, have been swallowed up by the small row-crop farms and the rambler-style houses built there since World War II.

Many of the older farmers who came to Washington on immigrant trains from the Midwest and cleared the land of sagebrush and bunchgrass with horses and muscle and sweat, do not like the emergence of agriculture as an industry. To them the family farm, not the family corporation, was an honorable way of life. It was a life centered around family cooperation, of parents knowing exactly where their children were at any given hour of the day. It was a time when girls could cook, clean house, do chores and take care of an entire family long before puberty. It was a time when boys anticipated additional work responsibilities, when their approach to manhood was marked by the type of work he did, and getting to drive a tractor or a combine on equal terms with adults was part of the initiation ceremonies into manhood.

The aging farmers and ranchers understand their children's migration to the cities, and realize there is little other choice. But they do not necessarily like it. Today's farms with the one-man machinery has reduced the farm work force to a tenth the number needed before World War II. Income has not gone up proportionately, and the basic truth is that a farm which once would support a large family today will barely support two adults.

So the migration began, and a way of life, a traditional and useful way of life, faded with the migration. Lamentations are in order, but futile.

In the cities, behind desks with mounds of paper, are the men and women who remember a different life. Some believe it was a better life.

But they know they cannot return. The jobs are not there. The amenities of city life are absent. Solitude is abhorrent to most. So they keep their memories.

They remember that special feeling at the end of a long day in the fields when the day no longer is hot, only comfortable, and the thought of a shower, clean clothes and a hot, hearty dinner quickens the pace across the open fields to the house.

They remember the Grange dances where there were no strangers and boys pulled practical jokes on each other to compete for the attention of a girl. They remember the place names, the curves in every road, the landmarks that might be a rock, a windmill, a patch of sand, a culvert or the design of a butte against the horizon.

They remember the still mornings and evenings when the sound of a screen door slamming or a windmill could be heard for miles. They remember sitting on the porch at night watching the stars appear overhead and miles away the lights going on in a neighbor's house.

No matter how long they live in the cities or how far they progress in their careers, those things they remember will always represent home.

On pages 52 and 53 preceding: Light dusting of snow defines
furrows of winter wheat on the rolling hills near Dayton.
Abandoned farm structures dot the Eastern Washington
countryside adding a touch of nostalgia.

Late afternoon sun renders a near-perfect silhouette
in a cornfield near La Conner.

Irrigation water has transformed desert sand dunes
into rich farmland in the Columbia Basin.

Modern potato harvester at work in the
Columbia Basin.

Horses graze peacefully on pastureland in an
Eastern Washington valley.

Spring thaw comes to a snow-bound ranch
in the Klickitat Valley.

Small field of winter wheat in the Touchet River
Valley near the Blue Mountains.

Cowboys bring herd of Hereford cattle down slopes of
the North Cascades into Okanagon ranch country.

Okanagon River near its confluence with the
Columbia River.

## THE SEASONS

To those who work the land, spring has a loose alliance with the calendar: It begins the first day a plow can be taken into the fields to turn over last year's wheat stubble. Once spring comes, in March or April, the slow process of preparing the summer fallow for next fall's crop begins and the tractors with their rattling cabs that keep out the cold and rain slowly darken the fields, releasing the pungent odor of earth as the damp ground is turned.

Spring is plowing new ground, fertilizing the green new wheat. Then, when the days get longer and hotter, rod-weeding the summer fallow until it is a uniform tan, no green of weeds or of volunteer grain in sight.

Of all the spring work, rod-weeding is the most dramatic, dirty and representative of the season, and it is what one remembers most of that season. The prevailing southwest wind usually quits during the night and by morning when men go to the fields, they often see a sprinkle of dew glinting low on the wheat stalks, or accumulated into little drops where the heads emerge from the stalk; only enough moisture to weigh down the summer fallow without nourishing it. And by the time the men have finished servicing the equipment—pumping fuel into the tractor and greasing the weeders and checking them for needed repairs—they feel the first hint of a breeze coming up out of the southwest, little more than a subtle movement in the cool morning air, like a sleeping horse shifting his weight.

During the first time or two around the summer fallow there is very little dust. What does stir up hugs the ground or drifts a few feet and settles. But by midmorning the dew is gone, the wind hot and strong and the dust a cloud that envelopes the tractor, the driver and the rod-weeders.

Those early summer days are a time of each day being exactly like the last one, when the passage of time is measured by the amount of weeding accomplished and the amount remaining to be done. Only the cloud formations late in the day change. It is work at it simplest, and for one who can bear hours of solitude with the sound of a clattering tractor, it can be joy. For one who cannot bear his own company in a cloud of dust, it could be maddening.

During this time the landscape is one of shimmering heat waves and huge clouds of dust moving slowly back and forth from dawn to dusk. Inside each of these small duststorms is a man, a tractor and the equipment, usually more than 40 feet of the rod-weeders, those simple pieces of machinery peculiar to the Northwest wheat country that save farmers thousands of dollars each year. They are square-inch rods suspended from wheeled machines, geared so that they ride just beneath the surface of the loose soil. They turn in the opposite direction they are being pulled, turning up the weeds' roots, exposing them to the sun to die. It is far cheaper than spraying with chemicals, faster than hoeing and dirtier than both.

From midmorning until quitting time the driver finds himself in a swirling, choking cloud of dust so thick that the tractor must be stopped often in order to see the track left by the marking wheel.

By late May when the powdery soil is dried out, the whirlwinds begin appearing. One can count up to a dozen at a time, moving slowly across the land in stately dances, reaching several hundred feet into the air, straight as Greek columns. Although they are runty tornados, they are harmless.

The decline of spring is measured by the color of the wheat, and when it reaches its golden harvest color and the combines are ready for the fields and new tires put on the trucks and the grain beds installed, spring is over.

Summer begins the day the combine is driven into the ripe, brittle wheat, and harvest hasn't changed much since the days when there would be up to 50 men beneath the shade trees on courthouse lawns, in taverns and pool halls with standing room only toward closing time each night. Then the men would go to cheap hotel rooms, if they had the money. If they did not, they would sleep in their cars or on the grass of the courthouse or the railroad depot.

Early in the morning they would be back out again to keep the vigil, clothes a little more wrinkled, beards a little longer as they dug into their pockets for the last money they had. Sometimes one of the men who already had been in harvest elsewhere would buy

*Wheat, heads heavy with kernels, bends over on Eastern Washington farm.*

coffee and donuts for the others. It wasn't always generosity; he might be broke in a few days himself.

After breakfast, back to the courthouse lawn, the pool halls and taverns to wait for the heat of midday and a farmer to pull up and ask for a combine man, a tractor driver, a sack sewer or a truck driver. Or worst of all, he would need a man to scoop wheat in storage bins.

It was always a mystery where the men went who did not find jobs after the first crucial days of harvest. A few would hang around town after harvest began, waiting for someone to walk off the job or get fired. There were always more workers than jobs. Some might hire on to do chores at half the going wage for truck drivers, but room and board was part of the deal.

But harvest is different now. With new combines there is no need for most farm families to hire outsiders. The man will operate the combine and his wife and children drive the trucks.

Harvest is fun only in the remembering. In the two or three weeks it normally takes to harvest a crop, the farmer's entire income is earned and that is no joking matter. It is hot, hard, nerve-wracking work when you worry about keeping the combine header high enough so too much stalk won't be cut by the sickle and low enough to catch every head of wheat; when every belt, chain and gear in the combine must be checked carefully two or three times a day to prevent costly breakdowns in the field; when, if possible, the combine isn't stopped to dump its load of wheat into the truck, and the truck driver must pull up beside the moving combine, match its speed and course until the combine's bulk tank is empty.

The Northwest is famous for its steep, rolling hills that were brutal for horses pulling combines. And it was here that the self-leveling combines were developed and the leveling devices were invented in the small town of Palouse.

When the last stalk of wheat has been cut and threshed, the last truckload of wheat delivered to the elevator, the combine is parked in the place it occupies eleven months of the year—then summer ends.

The weather is still hot and dry and will remain so for another month or two, but autumn begins the day after harvest. With the arrival of autumn, the field chores are few except for the all-important seeding of next year's crops in the summer fallow that was worked last spring. The fields of wheat stubble might be chiseled—cultivated with a deep-probing, narrow plow to loosen the soil for moisture storage during the winter. But the worst of the work is over.

In the fall and early winter the fields of the wheat country take on a shaggy look, like an animal growing its heavy winter coat. The yellow stubble turns a mottled brown. Trucks and the combine have left a maze of tracks in the flattened stubble. Patches of straw and chaff dot the rolling land.

Adjoining fields are neat and orderly, laid out in long, curving rows of next year's crop which by winter stands four or five inches tall, green and tender as grass, waiting for the cold of winter when it will become dormant to sit out the winter snow and frozen ground until growing season in the spring.

In the fall the wheat country is whatever you choose to call it. To some it is bleak and depressing—the wind blowing constantly it seems, often bringing blinding duststorms, and the clouds more often heavy and flat rather than fluffy as in the summer.

But to others the wheat country has a subtlety of color and mood this time of year that compensates for the discomfort of the wind and the below-zero temperatures of midwinter. They see the narrow range of color from the yellow of still-standing stubble to the brown of the rotting stalks; the flat yellow sea of prairie grass on uncultivated land; the very delicate blues and greens and grays of sagebrush; the green and brown of the new wheat and the purple shadow of the distant Blue Mountains or the broad expansive Cascade Range.

There is no definite day when winter begins. The weather gradually turns cooler with morning frosts and ground fog, hot afternoons and cold nights. The wind blows harder, the color leaves the sky and the farmers begin talking about an "open winter," a winter without snow to protect the young wheat from freezing or windburn.

Winter, then, is an evolutionary process and one is unaware of it until one day someone says something about "last fall."

Automobile lights weave an intricate pattern on loops above Lewiston and Clarkston at the confluence of the Snake and Clearwater Rivers.

Wild flowers carpet a meadow on the summit dome
of Liberty Cap in the Glacier Park Wilderness.

Originally a trading post, Spokane blossomed
into a railroad hub and today is
a major metropolitan center
for the Inland Empire.

Potholes Reservoir Recreation Area created by O'Sullivan Dam
in the Columbia Basin. On pages 68 and 69 following:
Small herd of cattle appears oblivious to winter
in the Klickitat Valley.

Boundary Dam harnesses the water of the Pend
Oreille River just south of the Canadian border.

Lush Red Delicious apples ready for harvest
in Yakima Valley orchard.

## THE VISIT

We drove too far that day—from the meadows beneath Mount Adams down to the Columbia River, up the barren gorge to Maryhill Museum, then north through Goldendale and over Satus Pass and down into the incredibly green Yakima Valley. We stopped only occasionally to let the children romp or to have a snack.

We could have stopped that night in the Yakima Valley, but my wife has a fear of rattlesnakes (which I secretly share) and the valley and brown hills above it looked like rattlesnake country. So we kept going—across the appropriately named Rattlesnake Hills, through the Hanford Atomic Reservation and down to the Columbia River again. It was dark when we reached Othello and the motels were filled. We drove on into the night, due east now toward Washtucna.

We arrived very late and the children scattered in all directions into the moonless night while we rented a room at the only motel. I fell asleep while my wife was still bedding down the children and woke the next morning when one of them began marching back and forth across my midsection. I didn't want to get up because it meant the work of packing the clothes, rolling sleeping bags and cramming everything back into the car. But when I stepped outside I forgot the aches and pains. Although I was born elsewhere, that morning I felt as though I was home again.

From all outward appearances, Washtucna is just another small town with a railroad running through it and sidings that run past the grain elevators. It is hot in the summer, cold and virtually deserted on winter nights. In the opinion of many urbanites, it is a miserable place to visit but living there or in any of a hundred similar towns would be unthinkable.

Obviously I don't feel that way. It is something of my second home and some of the most pleasant summers of my life were spent working in the wheat harvest near there.

There had been a light rain the previous night and we could still smell it in the air and see it glinting on the sagebrush and leaves of the trees. The sky was overcast with a band of clear sky over the scabrock east of town, etching the landscape against the opening.

We drove the length of the broad street and it pleased me that little had changed. Memory tends to distort and places we once enjoyed are never the same after a long absence. But Washtucna was exactly as I remembered it.

Tic Connell was alive then and I always bought gas from him, in part because I operated his service station one summer while he went on vacation, and because I always appreciated his greeting when I returned from a year's absence:

"Hi. What'll you have?"

None of the usual "How've you been?" "About time you got back." "How do you like things over on the coast?"

With Tic it was as though I had never been away, or at the most, had been out on the farm the past week. It was a relief after answering the same questions over and over.

This time, however, we stopped at Tom Hays' station because he had bought it since my last visit and also because I wanted to see if he would really tell my wife (who had never met him) all those lies and half-lies he had concocted about my bachelor days over there.

But Tom was a gentleman and gave me a pained look when I accused him of speaking poorly of me in my absence.

"I'd never tell lies about you," he protested, and gave Bill West, another old friend, an exaggerated wink. It was no accident that my wife saw the wink.

There were a few new faces in familiar places in town. Frank Stewart had bought Kenny Day's drugstore and relinquished the liquor license, much to the pleasure of Morris Moline, who now owned the hardware store across the street and possessed the liquor license. Tony Dirks, a handsome young man who was causing high-school girls' adrenalin to pump when I left, now was married to a girl as pretty as he was handsome and they owned the grocery store and butcher shop. Tony was making specialty sausages and shipping them all over the country.

Then we drove down to Palouse Falls, which in late summer was the equivalent of a leaky faucet, but beautiful as only massive rock formations can be. We drove back to Washtucna and down the narrow highway across the old Mullan Road toward Benge, winding down draws between fields of summer fallow and stubble and finally down a steep hill to Cow Creek and the lush meadows it nourishes.

At Benge we headed back west across the Harder Ranch and up to the wheat plateau again and cut across the high plain on a dirt road toward Chet and Pearl Bell's farm. Clusters of farm buildings were dotted across the fields almost at random, it seemed, and stood out against the darkening sky like convoys riding the crest of huge waves of earth.

The Bells weren't home when we arrived, so we went in and made ourselves at home as we would never do in any other home. My wife prepared dinner for the children and I took them out for a walk in the stubble field, land over which I had driven a tractor dozens of times. Soon they were playing a running game with the Bells' slightly wacky Cocker Spaniel, Bobo. Suddenly his attention was turned to a mole hole and he began digging with great industry. The children made the mistake of standing at the business end of the excavation and were covered with that fine Adams County dirt.

Shortly after dinner the doorbell rang, and we were not at all surprised to discover the Bells standing outside their own door, waiting for us to welcome them in.

They never seem to change. Once in a great while we write, usually a brief letter or a Christmas card. But most of the time we assume they are doing nicely, as they do us, and we pop in on each other whenever we're of a mind to.

They live a good life. They have problems shared by the rest of humanity, but there is an order to their lives unlike anyone else I know. Part of it may be attributed to the life of all farmers who live by the dictates of the seasons and the weather and the health of the crops they grow. But I suspect it also is because they live the life they want to live and are not wasting it with envying cattle ranchers, row-crop farmers or city dwellers. We stayed up late that night bringing each other up to date on our lives. We slept soundly and woke rested.

The next morning we packed after a brief visit with other friends and prepared to return to Western Washington. Then Chet asked the question that always makes the trip a little easier:

"Well, when are you coming home again?"

The Palouse River plunges over a high lava cliff
in Palouse Falls State Park.

Autumn-tinted vine maple along a logging road in
Gifford Pinchot National Forest lends unusual
contrast to Mt. Adams.

Indians race down a steep slope into Okanagon River
as climax to famous Omak Stampede. Wild roses in
the Pend Oreille River valley. Grand Coulee Dam
on the Columbia River.

The Wenatchee River roaring through Tumwater Canyon on the eastern slope of the Cascade Range.

Spring-blooming lupin and balsam root carpet the
rolling hills near the Columbia River.

Peach blossoms herald the coming of spring
to a Yakima Valley orchard.

Fir trees frame Mt. Rainier bathed in a soft glow
of the setting sun.

Autumn colors clearly defined on vine maple foliage.
On pages 84 and 85 following: Winter reflections
on the Wenatchee River near Leavenworth.

A stream cascades through a forest-bound
corridor in Gifford-Pinchot National Forest.

## THE NETTERS

A light rain had been falling off and on for several days and the sun hadn't been seen for at least a week. Ask a man when he had last seen his shadow and he would think a moment, then shrug. It was winter. Gray, dripping days are normal on the Lower Columbia River.

A group of commercial fishermen lounged around the pot-bellied stove in an old cannery building in Cathlamet. When they went to the coffee pot on the stove, their movements were the unhurried, deliberate motions of men accustomed to working according to the cycles of the tides. They knew how to wait and they could occupy themselves with long periods of silence punctuated by an occasional yarn, usually told at their own expense.

The cannery building was at least seventy years old, perhaps older. It made no difference. Craftsmen built it and it would stand several more decades with only token repairs. The canning machinery had been removed years before, but the owner permitted gillnet fishermen to stow their gear in the cavernous building, repair boats and use it as a combination workshop and clubhouse. It smelled faintly of fish, but stronger of gasoline and oil, of new wood where a boat was being repaired and that peculiar mixture of salt and freshwater that permeates the Lower Columbia.

Just after dark the tide began ebbing and although the ocean is more than fifty miles away, the river began dropping and the current moving westward again. Some of the salty tang seemed to move away with the current. Men began leaving the cannery, climbing down wooden ladders into their waiting boats. With a gurgling roar, the engines kicked over and the boats pulled away into the broad, dark river.

Within an hour the fishermen had strung their nets out behind the boats, several hundred feet with lead weights at the bottom and wooden or plastic floats on the top. At one end was a small, square float with a battery-powered light. At the other end was the low-slung gillnet boat, built on the Columbia River by men who knew the best design for the river. Physics, learned by experience rather than by book, dictated that both ends of the nets would drift down the river at exactly the same rate of speed. Hopefully, salmon migrating upstream would entangle themselves in the net, hooking their gills in the mesh.

At the end of each fisherman's drifting zone, or "set," they began hauling in the net, a floodlight illuminating the rear of the boat so they could clean debris and salmon from the net as it was reeled aboard. Some fishermen were lucky. Others came back to the cannery early the next morning with the tide change empty-handed.

Gillnetters are a diminishing breed on the Columbia, as are the fish they seek. The salmon has been called the most highly subsidized creature in the Northwest with the network of hatcheries along the Columbia's tributaries and the millions of dollars spent each year rearing them or trying to improve methods of rearing them. Like the bald eagle, our national symbol, the salmon is the symbol for many of the Northwest. It, too, is an endangered species.

All along the Lower Columbia the old cannery buildings perch out over the water, visible memories of another time. The older one becomes, the more pleasant those other times seem. There were canneries at Stella, at Brookfield, at Skamokawa, Pillar Rock and Altoona. One of the largest was at Knappton, which today has a maze of piling stubs protruding from the river's edge as reminders of the docks and the complex of buildings that once stood over the water. Here the Chinese workers were brought to receive low pay and long hours in the canneries. Parts of the buildings still stand above the water, but piece by piece they drop into the river each year and float out to sea.

As one nears the mouth of the Columbia it becomes wider until it is seven miles or more across, and during storms it has waves similar to those on the open ocean a few miles away. It was on this stretch of river that the nation's most famous explorers, Lewis and Clark, camped and thought they were on an ocean beach. It was here that the immigrants from Scandinavia came because it reminded them so much of home.

Today the salmon are virtually gone, and with their passing goes the gillnetters and their towns. In place of the fishing villages are a series of parks, some in existence now and others in the proposal stage. The rare Columbia white-tail deer now have their own private refuge, which they share peacefully with dairy cattle between Cathlamet and Skamokawa. Migratory waterfowl have a refuge near Ridgefield. State and federal agencies have proposed a chain of parks on islands in the river that will bring boaters to the river in increasing numbers.

But the Lower Columbia retains much of its charm, and this is nowhere more apparent than on Puget Island near Cathlamet. From the highway above the river the island appears nondescript, and few people visit it while driving to or from the ocean beaches. But once on the island, one is charmed by its mixture of agriculture and fishing. Diked sloughs that look like canals lace the island and are named for practical or emotional reasons—Steamboat and Welcome for example. The island is protected from the Columbia's floods by a series of high dikes with roads atop them and the farms and irrigation ditches are as orderly as the farmlands the immigrants left one or two generations ago to come to America.

Near the Cowlitz-Wahkiakum County line is a stretch of beach jutting out in to the river beside the highway where it was carved from the base of a sheer cliff. It is a favorite picnic spot during the summer months, and the year around is used by fishermen. They cast their bait far out into the river, prop their poles or clamp them to a log, hang a bell on the tip and gather around a fire or in a car to chat and wait for the bell to sound. Many of the fishermen are retired and use the beach as a social center, and the area has been dubbed Social Security Beach by local wags.

One wet winter day one man was sitting all alone on the beach, a poncho draped over him and a charcoal fire in a bucket between his feet. The fish were not biting, and he had just drank the last of his coffee from a thermos. He doused the fire with river water and loaded his gear into the car.

Just before he drove away, he turned to a bystander who watched the tired, wet old man from the comfort of his car. "It may not look like it, but it was fun," he said, then drove away.

The bystander looked at the beach, the steady rain, the swift, dark river and felt cold and wet. But he admired the old man who apparently had spent his working years in the Lower Columbia weather and said it was fun to sit in the cold and the rain and not catch a fish.

Puget Island in the Lower Columbia River.
Rest area on State Highway 14
overlooking the Columbia River near Lyle.

The Wind River nursery, birthplace of millions
of evergreen trees.

Skamokawa Harbor on the Lower Columbia.

Morning sun accentuates the weathered piling,
remnants of major fishing center at Knappton
near mouth of Columbia River.

Ominous April clouds add beauty to a field of
daffodils in Columbia River bottomland.

Perhaps the last covered bridge in use in the
state spans Grays River.

The Columbia River as it enters the gorge near
White Salmon. Fisherman at peace with the world
in the clear water of the Kalama River.

## THE HIKE

It wasn't a difficult hike—only seven miles round trip. A member of the backpacking aristocracy would scoff at it, and as he reads these words he might wonder why the bother to write them. But for us it was sufficient.

Unless other hikers had ignored the signup sheet in a box at the trail head, we were only the second party making the hike all summer. The trail was in excellent condition and no footprints were ahead of us. The low spots in the trail were moss-covered, and the switchbacks showed neither erosion nor abuse by hikers cutting across them.

We started at a lake and in less than ten feet from water's edge we were in the absolute silence of the cool forest. The trees were all second-growth and hadn't shut out enough sun to kill the berries and brush beneath them. An occasional vine maple caught the sunlight on its broad, bright leaves.

The trail was unrelentingly uphill, and we stopped frequently to rest, leaning against the bank or sitting on a fallen tree that had spanned the trail before chain saws had opened the trail again.

The children were alternately enthralled or so fatigued they couldn't climb another step. We bullied and joked them ahead to the next turn or the next stump for a rest. We told them there were streams ahead and hoped we were right. We were. The first was hardly more than a steep trickle but enough to mix a half-gallon of orange drink, which we savored with the packs off. The children made a miraculous recovery. Their fatigue vanished and they scampered up and down the steep ravine beside the stream, leaping across it, drinking noisily from their cupped palms.

The burst of energy was immediately deflated when we told them it was pack time again. But onward and upward we trudged, hoping we were actually farther than the two-mile post said we were.

The steep trail continued its climb, back and forth on the switchbacks, along the face of wooded hillsides. Then another stream, this one larger, noisier and with more room for the children to play during the second miraculous recovery from exhaustion.

Shortly after leaving the last stream, we came to the first real opening in the forest. It was a slide area, where nothing grew except weeds. Below us more than two thousand feet was the lake, purple in the atmospheric haze. Above us was another thousand feet of rotten hillside, scored by numerous small slides with a deep groove in the center from the last major slide. Directly ahead was the trail that looked like a chalk line drawn on a blackboard, then carelessly erased. Hoping we seemed calm, we clutched the children's hands and began inching across, neither of us admitting to fear but both expecting the loose earth to suddenly begin sliding toward the lake, taking us with it. The children were careful but calm; the parents were careful but certainly not calm. The children were surprised when a rest stop was called just beyond the slide without their having to demand it.

Just beyond the slide the forest changed dramatically. Across a line almost as definite as a power-line right-of-way, we were in a forest of gigantic Douglas fir that had never been subjected to a timber cruiser or a thinning crew. There no longer was underbrush— only Douglas fir. Nurse logs lay scattered at random, covered with moss and seedlings attempting to emulate their elders. The forest was a study in light. Bold shafts of sun penetrated occasionally like floodlights in a darkened theatre. The odor was different, too. We smelled that curious combination of decay and greenery, of life and death. We knew that for the first time since the hike began, we were amid a forest that was alive when our calendars began.

The trail was still steep, but the sudden change refreshed us and we found ourselves speaking in lower tones. Sound carried farther and we could speak in a stage whisper and be heard from front to rear of our column.

Our objective now was less than a mile away, and the packs no longer felt so heavy. The air was cooler here and the switchbacks less difficult.

We emerged from the forest and crossed a sharp ridge that opened up the view in both directions. Far below was the saltwater. On the other side was a series of foothills, then jutting up behind them, as if painted there, were the peaks, pure white; the lower mountains a variegated green. The only haze was between us and the lake directly below, and far out over the saltwater.

Now there was less than a half mile to go. Ahead was the last of the climb, down into the forest again, around an outcropping of rocks, then up a steep trail with no switchbacks because there was no room for them.

Soon we were on an almost vertical stretch, then suddenly one of the children shouted: "We're here!" The others dropped their knapsacks and stampeded up to the summit.

Trees and old snags hung onto the summit precariously, and boulders large as a tractor were scattered around the pinnacle. We were not near timberline at the top of the small mountain, but we didn't care. We had set an objective and reached it.

We sat on rocks and looked down on earth and up at the sky. We cooled off from the climb and said it would be worth the effort even if it were twice as far. Then we went back to more level ground for lunch.

The sun was dropping close to the sea when we cleaned up the picnic area and started downhill. Where we had to cajole and threaten our brood to move before, we now had to cajole, threaten and even frighten them to walk, not run, and to stay together. But they broke and ran down one rise, up another and then out of sight.

Then we heard one "Uh oh!" loudly.

They had reached the slide, and we found them nose to neck staring at the open space beneath them as if transfixed. We joined hands again and shuffled slowly across.

The rest of the trip was anticlimactic until the youngest discovered it was close to dinner time and that starvation was imminent. With a combination of reason and nonsense, the emaciated sibling was bilked into walking the rest of the way to the car without being carried.

The purist backpacker, those who think anything less than three days in the wilderness is an urban stroll, may not be impressed with a hike of this nature.

But the children were and they still remember it although they have done other things involving more stamina and greater distances, more danger and more discomfort. They remember the cathedral setting of the virgin timber, the small, pure streams, the slide area and the silence of the summit.

We like to think of the hike as more of a cultural outing than a physical activity.

Image Lake at base of Glacier Peak
in Glacier Peak Wilderness.

Wild Rose in the Pend Oreille River Valley.

Right: Looking north across the international
boundary from the crest of Winchester Mountain in
Mt. Baker National Forest. Peaks from left to right
include Canadian Border, American Border
and Mt. Larrabee.

Campers enjoy a blazing campfire in Goat Rocks
Wilderness Area. In background, Mt. Adams.

On pages 100 and 101 preceding: Magic Mountain
dominates a trail down Sahale Arm in the North
Cascades National Park. Doubtful Lake nestles in a
glacier-carved cirque on the slopes of Sahale Mountain
in the North Cascades National Park.

Spectacular glaciers hang on the upper slopes of
Forbidden Peak in the North Cascades National Park.

Climbers scale the slopes of the North Central
Cascades. Salmon leaps a waterfall on the Soleduck
River and Lady fern and Maidenhair fern flourish
on the slopes of Mt. Hamilton.

Inspiration and Perfection Lakes, two of several
Enchantment Lakes in a high plateau basin
on the crest of Stuart Range. In background
Prusig Peak and The Temple.

Buck Creek follows a boulder-strewn course
through a dense forest in the North Cascades.

## THE SOUND

Suddenly the sun was up, ricocheting off the city buildings, breaking into shards of light that lay on the flat water as the tug moved along the waterfront. The buildings looked new and shiny with the strong light revealing form rather than texture, and the mountains surrounding Puget Sound on three sides made Puget Sound feel like the surface of liquid in a bowl.

The men on the tug had seen dawn from sea level too many times to be awed, and they went about their work with professional simplicity, each thankful the winter day was warm and light. They had been wet and cold so often they no longer complained. Being practical men, they wasted no breath worrying about something over which they had no control or influence. Foul weather was as much a part of their life as payday.

It was an "inside" tug as differentiated from an "outside" or sea-going vessel. They worked two-week tours of duty, then had two weeks ashore at home. It kept them away from home half of the year but it also gave them the other half without having to leave home at all. They liked the arrangement and said their families did, too.

Points, bays, inlets, rocks and passages were to them what street addresses and towns are to the landlocked. Their social center was the galley, where a pot of coffee was always ready and they held the heavy white mugs cupped in their hands, ignoring the handles.

They told good stories, underplaying them as if they feared being accused of telling "sea stories." They told of the days before radar, sonar, two-way radios and other gadgets on which they rely so heavily today. They told of using the whistle to judge distances from other vessels and the shore during heavy fog. The trip through Deception Pass was especially tricky without instruments because the cross currents could slap a vessel against the cliffs before the crew knew they had lost headway. A skipper would use the whistle constantly, ear tuned to the echo to translate the time between the whistle and the echo into distance.

Puget Sound for them is a highway, a place of business where they spend half of their working lives, usually beginning as young deckhands and progressing up the chain of command through experience, classroom work, books and Coast Guard examinations.

But their use of the Sound is only one of hundreds, and each user has a selfish interest in it. There are commercial fishermen who worry about the purity of the water and the number of sports fishermen competing for the salmon, and the sports fishermen worry about the number of commercial licenses granted each year and the number of days commercial nets are permitted. Oceanographers use the Sound as a vast laboratory. Marine biologists study its underwater residents and their fluctuating population. Sailing enthusiasts worry about the heavy shipping traffic and ship's pilots ponder the mathematical probability that one day they will be in charge of a vessel that runs down a small pleasure craft.

But most Puget Sound Basin residents and visitors enjoy the Sound from its shoreline. Property laws permit no-trespassing signs between shoreline homes and the high-tide mark, and those without either waterfront or view homes must either look at it from the waterfront parks scattered around the Sound, or from public property on hills surrounding the water. Use of this gentle body of water and its shoreline has become rather exclusive.

But when one does go to its shoreline, no matter the season, it is an experience that should be repeated several times a year. There is a mystical quality about large bodies of saltwater lacking in freshwater lakes or rivers. There is no actual boundaries to saltwater and it represents one natural resource on the planet we probably will never completely control; we can enjoy it, pollute it, use it but we will never master it.

Storms do wrack the Sound, making it unsafe for small boats, but its general demeanor is one of gentleness, calm beauty and peace. It is noted at its southern end for the clusters of islands ranging from the urbanized Bainbridge Island to the virgin beauty of Squaxin Island near Olympia. Actually a reservation for a small Indian tribe, Squaxin Island is one of those beautiful places the treaty signers somehow missed while attempting to take the best land for the exclusive use of new settlers more than a century ago. In keeping with the white man's great urge for land ownership, there have been repeated efforts by realtors and legislators to gain some kind of control over the island. Instead, the Indians have resisted and are keeping it for their exclusive use.

Squaxin Island doesn't look that much different than other islands in Puget Sound—low, wooded with a few stretches of fine sandy beach and other sections with a bank dropping directly into the water. But that is at once the island's charm and the other island's misfortune. Squaxin Island is an example of good management, because it is still in its natural, undeveloped, state; other islands have been "developed" and not always with wisdom or a concern for beauty. While the signs preventing use by the public are an irritant to those who do not own waterfront property in the Sound, they also can be a form of protection against overuse or demolition of the natural growth that protects the shorelines.

If Washington has a never-never land, it is the San Juan Islands, far enough from the population centers to offer privacy to its residents, but not so far that they cannot be visited on a weekend or vacation. San Juan Islanders are prone to considering themselves citizens of another country, part American, part Canadian, but actually neither. They tolerate the rest of Washington, but ignore it as much as possible. Each island has its own distinct character, both in the kind of residents each attracts and in the terrain of each island. Some are virtually arid, devoid of heavy timber or bushes; others are almost rain forests. Some are rocky, others have excellent soil. Some are quite heavily populated by Canadians, others have numerous Greek families on them. Artists, novelists and retired actors move there, and airline pilots commute to Seattle as casually as others commute a few miles by car.

The Puget Sound Basin remains one of the state's most beautiful areas in spite of the heavy population it has attracted, at least in part because of that beauty. When one can begin the working day with views of Mount Rainier, the Cascades, the Olympics and Puget Sound, plus the numerous lakes and rivers, it may not make the prospect of another desk-bound day any more attractive than a desk-bound day in the desert or the Great Plains. But knowing those things are there and that they are available on the weekends eases the burden of having to work.

One must admit there are far less interesting places in the world to live or to visit.

Ketch rides at anchor off a private dock on Lake
Washington. In background, Mt. Rainier.

Colorful rainbow arches through the mist at base of
Snoqualmie Falls near Seattle.

Sunset silhouettes bridge spanning Deception Pass
between Fidalgo and Whidbey Islands.

Field of Hyacinths in the Puyallup Valley.

Aerial view of Sucia Island, in the San Juans, reveals its
picturesque peninsulas and snug harbors.

Left: Old contorted maple trees draped in moss in
the Olympic National Park's rain forest.

Remnants of winter snow greet early summer visitors on
Hurricane Ridge in Olympic Mountains near Port Angeles.

Offshore rocks at Point of Arches along the remote
shoreline of the Olympic Peninsula.

Lighthouse atop Cape Disappointment near
mouth of Columbia River.

Shoreline of Fort Canby State Park offers a spectacular
view of North Head Lighthouse.

Spectacular Soleduck Falls in the Olympic
National Park's rain forest.

Right: Low tide unveils marine gardens, surf-sculptured offshore rocks at base of Cape Flattery.

Dense early morning fog hangs heavy over fishing
boats moored in harbor at Westport.

Right: Morning sun silhouettes rocks along
the coast near Point Grenville.

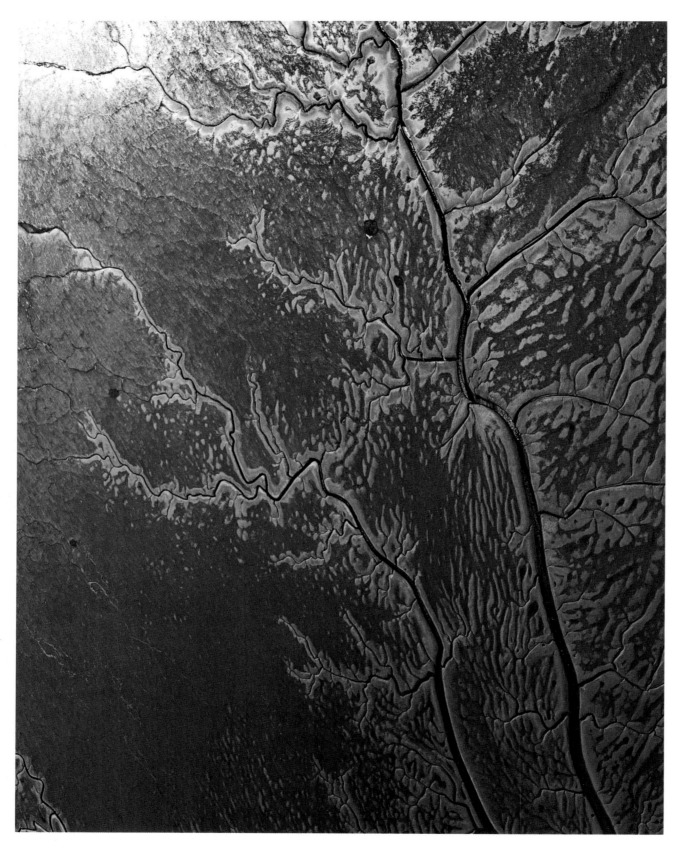

Aerial view at low tide in Grays Harbor creates
an abstract pattern.